KISS A FROG!

Make Me Laugh!

KISS A FROG!
jokes about fairy tales, knights, and dragons

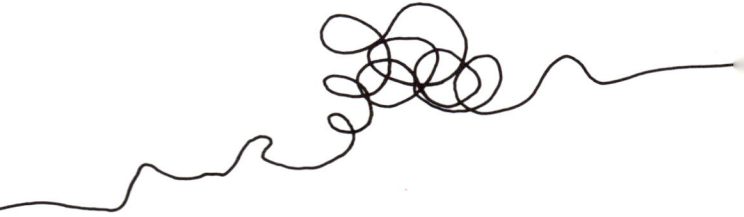

by Rick & Ann Walton / pictures by Joan Hanson

Lerner Publications Company · Minneapolis

Copyright © 1989 by Lerner Publications Company

All rights reserved. International copyright secured.
No part of this book may be reproduced in any form
whatsoever without permission in writing from the publisher
except for the inclusion of brief quotations in an
acknowledged review.

Library of Congress Cataloging-in-Publication Data

Walton, Rick.
  Kiss a frog.

  (Make me laugh!)
  Summary: A collection of jokes featuring characters
from fairy tales.
  1. Fairy tales—Juvenile humor. 2. Knights and
knighthood—Juvenile humor. 3. Dragons—Juvenile
humor. 4. Wit and humor, Juvenile. [1. Fairy tales—
Wit and humor. 2. Knights and knighthood—Wit and
humor. 3. Dragons—Wit and homor. 4. Jokes]
I. Walton, Ann, 1963- . II. Hanson, Joan, ill.
III. Title. IV. Series.
PN6231.F285W35   1989   818'5402   88-13134
ISBN 0-8225-0970-9

Manufactured in the United States of America

2 3 4 5 6 7 8 9 10 98 97 96 95 94 93 92 91 90 89

Q: How do you catch a fairy?
A: Grab its fairy tale.

Q: When were clocks invented?
A: Once upon a time.

Q: What race could neither the tortoise nor the hare enter?
A: The human race.

Q: Did the tortoise win the race by a long distance?
A: No, he won by a hare.

Q: How long was Cinderella's glass slipper?
A: One foot long.

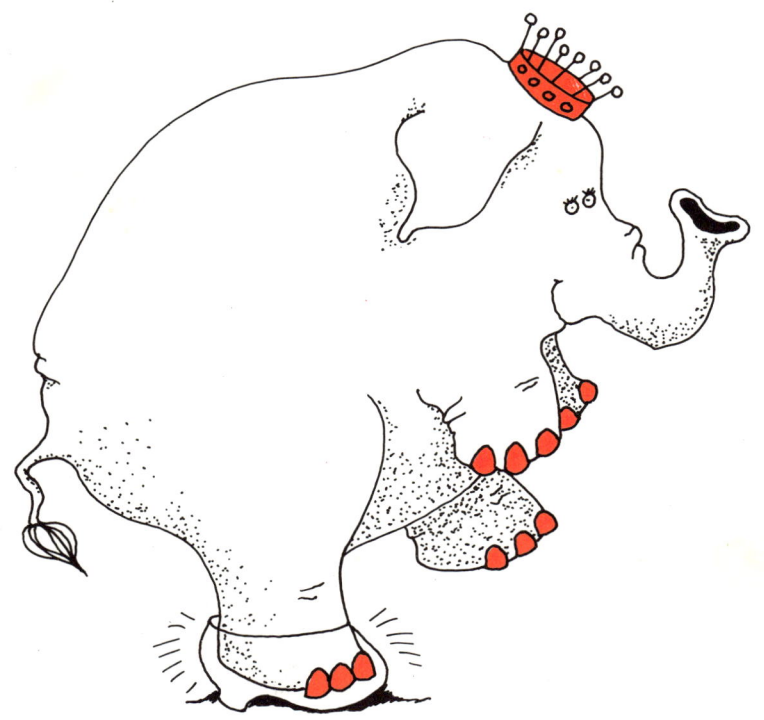

Q: Who had big ears, weighed seven thousand pounds, and married a handsome prince?
A: Cinderelephant.

Q: How do you fix a flat pumpkin?
A: With a pumpkin patch.

Q: Why did the ugly stepsister slap the glass slipper?
A: Because the slipper pinched her.

Q: What do you get when you cross the Frog Prince with Cinderella's footman?
A: Foot Prince.

Q: How did the elves stay awake to make shoes all night?
A: They used sole-r energy.

Q: Why did the elves make all right shoes?
A: Because they didn't want to make all wrong shoes.

Q: What fairy tale does your foot dream about when it falls asleep?
A: Sleeping Bootee.

Q: What fairy tale tells of a pretty girl who was ordered to clean house for a hundred years?
A: Sweeping Beauty.

Q: What's a pig's favorite fairy tale?
A: Slopping Beauty.

Q: Who is the loveliest lamb in all the fairy tales?
A: Sheeping Beauty.

Q: Why did Sleeping Beauty sleep for a hundred years?
A: Because her alarm clock was broken.

Q: Why didn't the princess sleep well on top of twenty mattresses?
A: Would you sleep well if you could fall that far when you rolled out of bed?

Q: Why did the queen decide to put a pea under the mattresses?
A: Because she was a pea-nut.

Q: What happened when Puss-in-Boots went to sea?
A: He became Puss-in-Boats.

Q: And what happened when a shark got him?
A: He became Puss-in-Bits.

Q: Why couldn't Tom Thumb play the piano?
A: Because he couldn't do the fingering.

Q: Why did the prince climb Rapunzel's hair?
A: Because the elevator was broken.

Q: How did Rapunzel become queen?
A: She was hair to the throne.

Q: Why was Rapunzel mad at the witch?
A: Because the witch kept getting in her hair.

Q: Why was the witch mad at Hansel and Gretel?
A: Because they were eating her out of house and home.

Q: Why was Little Red Riding Hood suspicious when she saw the wolf's big nose?
A: Because she knew that something smelled.

Q: What dragon ran around with Robin Hood?
A: Fire Tuck.

Q: What do you get when you cross Little Red Riding Hood with a bird?
A: Robin Hood.

Q: What wakes up a dragon in the morning?
A: The fire alarm.

Q: How do dragons weigh themselves?
A: On their scales.

Q: What do dragons do on their birthdays?
A: Light the candles, and the cake, and the presents...

Q: What dragon disappeared into thin air?
A: "Poof, the Magic Dragon."

Q: How do dragons swim?
A: They do the heat stroke.

Q: How do dentists fix dragons' teeth?
A: With a fire drill.

Q: What do dragons eat with their soup?
A: Firecrackers.

Q: Why are boring speeches like dragons?
A: Because boring speeches drag on, and on, and on...

Q: What do you get when a dragon jumps into the ocean?
A: A heat wave.

Q: What happens to a knight when a dragon breathes on him?
A: He ig-knights.

Q: Where do knights buy armor?
A: At a hard-wear store.

Q: Why shouldn't knights wear chain mail to fight a dragon?
A: Because dragons are chain smokers.

Q: When do dragons stop eating?
A: Mid-knight.

Q: What do you call a baby knight?
A: A knight crawler.

Q: What do you get when you cross a knight with a clown?
A: A court jouster.

Q: What kind of knight sings when the wind is blowing hard?
A: A knight-in-gale.

Q: What attracts knights in shining armor even more than fair maidens?
A: Magnets.

Q: When do most knights get hurt?
A: At knightfall.

Q: How do knights see in the dark?
A: They use knight lights.

Q: Where did the giant want to cook Jack?
A: In a jack pot.

Q: What did Jack's beanstalk grow?
A: Climb-a beans.

Q: What kind of locks won't keep people out of your house?
A: Goldi-locks.

Q: Why didn't the three bears eat their porridge?
A: Because they didn't have any mush-room.

Q: Why did the Baby Bear's chair break when Goldilocks sat on it?
A: Because it couldn't bear her weight.

Q: What did the first little pig say when the Big Bad Wolf blew down his house?
A: "That's the last straw!"

Q: Why did the Big Bad Wolf try to blow down the little pig's house?
A: Because he didn't have enough dynamite to blow it up.

Q: Why didn't the Three Billy Goats Gruff want to pay at the Troll Bridge?
A: Because it cost an arm and a leg.

Q: Why were the Billy Goats Gruff able to fool the Troll?
A: Because hungry Trolls will swallow anything.

ABOUT THE ARTIST

JOAN HANSON lives with her husband and two sons in Afton, Minnesota. Her distinctive, deliberately whimsical pen-and-ink drawings have illustrated more than 30 children's books. Hanson is also an accomplished weaver. A graduate of Carleton College, Hanson enjoys tennis, skiing, sailing, reading, traveling, and walking in the woods surrounding her home.

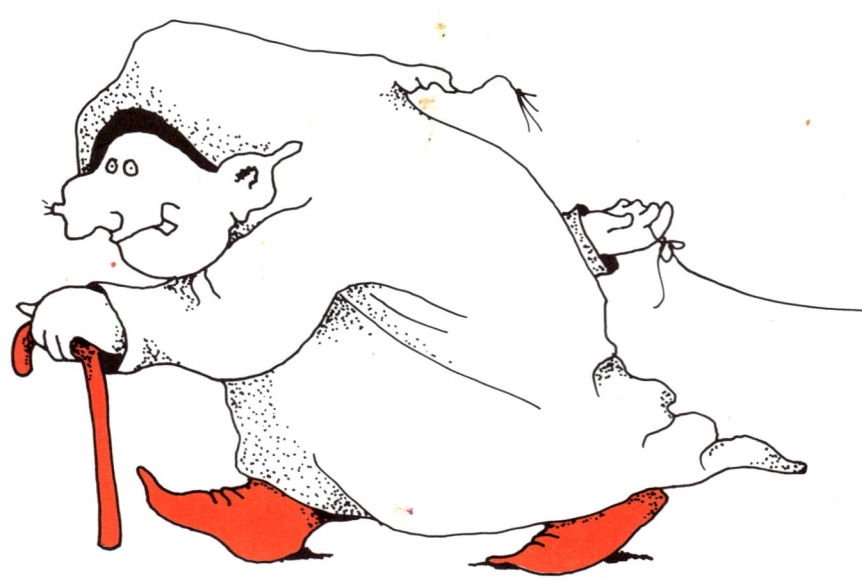

ABOUT THE AUTHORS

RICK AND ANN WALTON love to read, travel, play guitar, study foreign languages, and write for children. Rick also collects books and writes music while Ann knits and does origami. They are both graduates of Brigham Young University and live in Kearns, Utah, where Rick teaches sixth grade.

Make Me Laugh!

CAN YOU MATCH THIS?
CAT'S OUT OF THE BAG!
CLOWNING AROUND!
DUMB CLUCKS!
ELEPHANTS NEVER FORGET!
FACE THE MUSIC!
FOSSIL FOLLIES!
GO HOG WILD!
GOING BUGGY!
GRIN AND BEAR IT!
HAIL TO THE CHIEF!
IN THE DOGHOUSE!
KISS A FROG!
LET'S CELEBRATE!
OUT TO LUNCH!

OUT TO PASTURE!
SNAKES ALIVE!
SOMETHING'S FISHY!
SPACE OUT!
STICK OUT YOUR TONGUE!
WHAT A HAM!
WHAT'S YOUR NAME?
WHAT'S YOUR NAME, AGAIN?
101 ANIMAL JOKES
101 FAMILY JOKES
101 KNOCK-KNOCK JOKES
101 MONSTER JOKES
101 SCHOOL JOKES
101 SPORTS JOKES

1